LOVEROOT

BOOKS BY ERICA JONG

Loveroot (POETRY)
Fear of Flying (FICTION)
Half-Lives (POETRY)
Fruits & Vegetables (POETRY)

LOVEROOT
by Erica Jong

HOLT, RINEHART AND WINSTON   NEW YORK

reproduce

, Rinehart

Data

Jong, Erica.
Loveroot.

I. Title.
PS3560.O56L6   811'.5'4   74–15483
ISBN 0–03–014046–3

First Edition

Designer: Madelaine Caldiero

PRINTED IN THE UNITED STATES OF AMERICA

Some of these poems originally appeared in the following publications whose editors are thanked for permission to reprint:

About Women: An Anthology of Contemporary Fiction, Poetry, and Essays, edited by Stephen Berg and S. J. Marks, Fawcett, 1973: "Becoming a Nun"

American Poetry Review: "For Claudia, Against Narrowness," "Tachycardia," "The Insomniac Talks to God"

Beloit Poetry Journal: "Tapestry, with Unicorn" appeared in a somewhat different form under the name Erica Mann.

Columbia Forum: "Empty"

Encounter: "Egyptology," "Colder," "Parable of the Four-Poster"

Massachusetts Review: "Sylvia Plath Is Alive in Argentina"

Moonstruck: An Anthology of Lunar Poetry, edited by Robert Phillips, The Vanguard Press, 1973: "Dearest Man-in-the-Moon"

Mountain Moving Day: Poems by Women, edited by Elaine Gill, The Crossing Press, 1973: "Dearest Man-in-the-Moon," "Colder," "Sunjuice," "Dear Colette," "In the Penile Colony," "Becoming a Nun"

Ms.: "Dear Marys, Dear Mother, Dear Daughter"

The New Yorker: "Dear Keats"

The New York Times Magazine: "In Praise of Clothes"

Paris Review: "Wrinkles," "Becoming a Nun," "Testament (Or, Homage to Walt Whitman)"

Ramparts: "How-to Books & Other Absurdities," "Statue," "Insomnia & Poetry"

Redbook: "For My Husband," "Penis Envy"

Grateful acknowledgment is made to Houghton Mifflin Company for permission to reprint six lines from "Under the Maud Moon" by Galway Kinnell, from *The Book of Nightmares*, © 1971 by Galway Kinnell.

FOR LOUIS & BRYNA UNTERMEYER

> *Run mad as often as you choose,*
> *but do not faint.*
> —JANE AUSTEN

> *Je cognois tout, fors que moy mesmes.*
> —FRANÇOIS VILLON

> *What I claim is to live to the*
> *full the contradiction of my*
> *time, which may well make sarcasm*
> *the condition of truth.*
> —ROLAND BARTHES

CONTENTS

III / HUNGERING

I / MASH NOTES TO THE DEAD
& LETTERS TO THE LIVING

> . . . *I feel assured I should*
> *write from the mere yearning and*
> *fondness I have for the Beautiful*
> *even if my night's labours*
> *should be burnt every morning and*
> *no eye ever shine upon them.*
> *But even now I am perhaps not*
> *speaking from myself: but from*
> *some character in whose soul*
> *I now live.*
> —JOHN KEATS

Testament (Or, Homage to Walt Whitman)

> *loveroot, silkthread, crotch and vine . . .*
> —WALT WHITMAN

> *I trust all joy.*
> —THEODORE ROETHKE

I, Erica Jong, in the midst of my life,
    having had two parents, two sisters,
    two husbands, two books of poems
    & three decades of pain,

    having cried for those who did not love me
    & those who loved me—but not enough
    & those whom I did not love—
    declare myself now for joy.

There is pain enough to nourish us everywhere;
    it is joy that is scarce.

There are corpses piled up to the mountains,
    & tears to drown in,
    & bile enough to swallow all day long.

Rage is a common weed.
Anger is cheap.

Righteous indignation
    is the religion of the dead
    in the house of the dead
    where the dead speak to each other
    in creaking voices,

each arguing a more unhappy childhood
than the other.

Unhappiness is cheap.
    Childhood is a universal affliction.
    I say to hell with the analysts of minus & plus,
    the life-shrinkers, the diminishers of joy.

I say to hell with anyone
    who would suck on misery
    like a pacifier
    in a toothless mouth.
    I say to hell with gloom.

Gloom is cheap.
    Every night the earth resolves for darkness
    & then breaks its resolve
    in the morning.

Every night the demon lovers
    come with their black penises like tongues,
    with their double faces,
    & their cheating mouths
    & their glum religions of doom.

Doom is cheap.
    If the apocalypse is coming,
    let us wait for it in joy.

Let us not gnash our teeth
    on the molars of corpses—
    though the molars of corpses
    are plentiful enough.

Let us not scorn laughter
      though scorn is plentiful enough.

Let us laugh & bring plenty to the scorners—
      for they scorn themselves.

I myself have been a scorner
      & have chosen scornful men,
      men to echo all that was narrow in myself,
      men to hurt me as I hurt myself.

In my stinginess,
      my friends have been stingy.
In my narrowness,
      my men have been mean.

I resolve now for joy.

If that resolve means I must live alone,
      I accept aloneness.

If the joy house I inhabit must be
      a house of my own making,
      I accept that making.

No doom-saying, death-dealing, fucker of cunts
      can undo me now.

No joy-denyer can deny me now.
      For what I have is undeniable.
      I inhabit my own house,
      the house of my joy.

"Unscrew the locks from the doors!
Unscrew the doors themselves from their jambs!"

❦

Dear Walt Whitman,
     horny old nurse to pain,
     speaker of "passwords primeval,"
     merit-refuser, poet of body & soul—
     I scorned you at twenty
     but turn to you now
     in the fourth decade of my life,
     having grown straight enough
     to praise your straightness,
     & plain enough
     to speak to you plain
     & simple enough
     to praise your simplicity.

The doors open.
The metaphors themselves swing open wide!

Papers fall from my desk,
     my desk teeters on the edge of the cosmos,
     & I commit each word to fire.

I burn!
All night I write in suns across the page.
I fuel the "body electric" with midnight oil.
I write in neon sperm across the air.

❦

You were "hankering, gross, mystical, nude."
You astonished with the odor of your armpits.
You cocked your hat as you chose;

you cocked your cock—
but you knew "the Me myself."

You believed in your soul
      & believing, you made others
      believe in theirs.

The soul is contagious.
      One man catches another's
      like the plague;
      & we are all patient spiders
      to each other.

If we can spin the joythread
      & also catch it—

if we can be sufficient to ourselves,
      we need fear no entangling webs.

The loveroot will germinate.
The crotch will be a trellis for the vine,
      & our threads will all be intermingled silk.

How to spin joy out of an empty heart?
The joy-egg germinates even in despair.

Orgasms of gloom convulse the world;
      & the joy-seekers huddle together.

We meet on the pages of books & by beachwood fires.
We meet scrawled blackly in many-folded letters.
We know each other by free & generous hands.
We swing like spiders on each other's souls.

To Pablo Neruda

Again & again
I have read your books
without ever wishing to know you.

    I suck the alphabet of blood.
    I chew the iron filings of your words.
    I kiss your images like moist mouths
    while the black seeds of your syllables
    fly, fly, fly
    into my lungs.

Untranslated, untranslatable,
you are rooted inside me—
not you—but the you
of your poems:

    the man of his word,
    the lover who digs into the alien soil
    of one North American woman
    & plants a baby—
    love-child of Whitman
    crossed with the Spanish language,
    embryo, sapling, half-breed
    of my tongue.

            *

I saw you once—
your flesh—
at Columbia.
My alma mater
& you the visiting soul.

Buddha-like
you sat before a Buddha;
& the audience
craned its neck
to take you in.

Freak show—
visiting poet.
You sat clothed
in your thick
imperious flesh.

    I wanted to comfort you
    & not to stare.
    Our words knew each other.
    That was enough.

          ❧

Now you are dead
of fascism & cancer—
your books scattered,
the oil cruet on the floor.

    The sea surges through your house
    at Isla Negra,
    & the jackboots
    walk on water.

          ❧

Poet of cats & grapefruits,
of elephant saints;
poet of broken dishes
& Machu Picchu;
poet of panthers

& pantheresses;
poet of lemons,
poet of lemony light.

> The flies swarm
> thicker than print on a page,
> & poetry blackens
> like overripe bananas.
> The fascists you hated,
> the communists you loved,
> obscure the light, the lemons
> with their buzzing.

We were together
on the side of light.
We walked together
though we never met.
> The eyes are not political,
> nor the tastebuds,
> & the flesh tastes salty always
> like the sea;
> & the sea
> turns back the flies.

Dear Colette

Dear Colette,
I want to write to you
about being a woman
for that is what
you write to me.

I want to tell you how your face
enduring after thirty, forty, fifty . . .
hangs above my desk
like my own muse.

I want to tell you how your hands
reach out from your books
& seize my heart.

I want to tell you how your hair
electrifies my thoughts
like my own halo.

I want to tell you how your eyes
penetrate my fear
& make it melt.

I want to tell you
simply that I love you—
though you are "dead"
& I am still "alive."

&

Suicides & spinsters—
all our kind!

Even decorous Jane Austen
never marrying,
& Sappho leaping,
& Sylvia in the oven,
· & Anna Wickham, Tsvetaeva, Sara Teasdale,
& pale Virginia floating like Ophelia,
& Emily alone, alone, alone. . . .

But you endure & marry,
go on writing,
lose a husband, gain a husband,
go on writing,
sing & tap dance
& you go on writing,
have a child & still
you go on writing,
love a woman, love a man
& go on writing.
You endure your writing
& your life.

                    ✦

Dear Colette,
I only want to thank you:

for your eyes ringed
with bluest paint like bruises,
for your hair gathering sparks
like brush fire,
for your hands which never willingly
let go,
for your years, your child, your lovers,
all your books. . . .

Dear Colette,
you hold me
to this life.

Dear Marys, Dear Mother, Dear Daughter

Mary Wollstonecraft Godwin
Author of
A Vindication
Of the Rights of Woman:
Born 27 April, 1759:
Died 10 September, 1797
    —MARY WOLLSTONECRAFT'S
    GRAVESTONE, PLACED BY
    WILLIAM GODWIN, 1798

I was lonesome as a Crusoe.
    —MARY SHELLEY

It is all over,
little one, the flipping
and overleaping, the watery
somersaulting alone in the oneness
under the hill, under
the old, lonely bellybutton . . .
    —GALWAY KINNELL

What terrified me will terrify others . . .
    —MARY SHELLEY

1 / NEEDLEPOINT

Mothers & daughters . . .
something sharp
catches in my throat
as I watch my mother
nervous before flight,

do needlepoint—
blue irises & yellow daffodils
against a stippled woolen sky.

She pushes the needle
in & out
as she once pushed me:
sharp needle to the canvas of her life—
embroidering her faults
in prose & poetry,
writing the fiction
of my bitterness,
the poems of my need.

"You hate me," she accuses,
needle poised,
"why not admit it?"

I shake my head.
The air is thick
with love gone bad,
the odor of old blood.

If I were small enough
I would suck your breast . . .
but I say nothing,
big mouth,
filled with poems.

Whatever love is made of—
wool, blood, Sunday lamb,
books of verse
with violets crushed
between the pages,

tea with herbs,
lemon juice for hair,
portraits sketched of me asleep
at nine months old—
this twisted skein
of multicolored wool,
this dappled canvas
or this page of print
joins us
like the twisted purple cord
through which we first pulsed poems.

Mother, what I feel for you
is more
& less
than love.

2 / MARY WOLLSTONECRAFT GODWIN & MARY GODWIN SHELLEY

She was "lonesome
as a Crusoe,"
orphaned by childbirth,
orphaned being born,
killing her mother
with a stubborn afterbirth—
the medium they'd shared. . . .

Puppies were brought
to draw off Mary's milk,
& baby Mary screamed.

She grew up
to marry Shelley,
have four babes

(of whom three died)—
& one immortal monster.

Byron & Shelley
strutted near the lake
& wrote their poems
on purest alpine air.
The women had their pregnancies
& fears.

They bore the babies,
copied manuscripts,
& listened to the talk
that love was "free."

The brotherhood of man
did not apply:
all they contributed
to life
was life.

& Doctor Frankenstein
was punished
for his pride:
the hubris of a man
creating life.
He reared a wretched
animated corpse—
& Shelley praised the book
but missed the point.

Who were these gothic monsters?
Merely men.
Self-exiled Byron

with his Mistress Fame,
& Percy Shelley
with his brains aboil,
the seaman
who had never learned to swim.

Dear Marys,
it was clear
that you were truer.
Daughters of daughters,
mothers of future mothers,
you sought to soar
beyond complaints
of woman's lot—
& died in childbirth
for the Rights of Man.

3 / EXILES

This was the sharpness
of my mother's lesson.
Being a woman
meant eternal strife.
No colored wool could stitch
the trouble up;
no needlepoint
could cover it with flowers.

When Byron played
the exiled wanderer,
he left his ladies
pregnant or in ruin.
He left his children
fatherless for fame,

then wrote great letters
theorizing pain.

He scarcely knew
his daughters any more
than Mary knew the Mary
who expired
giving her birth.

All that remained in him:
a hollow loneliness
about the heart,
the milkless tug of memory,
the singleness of creatures
who breathe air.

Birth is the start
of loneliness
& loneliness the start
of poetry:
that seems a crude
reduction of it all,
but truth
is often crude.

& so I dream
of daughters
as a man might dream
of giving birth,
& as my mother dreamed
of daughters
& had three—
none of them her dream.

& I reach out for love
to other women
while my real mother
pines for me
& I pine for her,
knowing I would have to be
smaller than a needle
pierced with wool
to pierce the canvas of her life
again.

4 / DEAR DAUGHTER

Will you change all this
by my having you,
& by your having everything—
Don Juan's exuberance,
Childe Harold's pilgrimage,
books & babies,
recipes & riots?

Probably not.

In making daughters
there is so much needlepoint,
so much doing & undoing,
so much yearning—
that the finished pattern cannot please.

My poems will have daughters
everywhere,
but my own daughter
will have to grow
into her energy.

I will not call her Mary
or Erica.
She will shape
a wholly separate name.

& if her finger falters
on the needle,
& if she ever needs to say
she hates me,
& if she loathes poetry
& loves to whistle,
& if she never
calls me Mother,
she will always be my daughter—
my filament of soul
that flew,
& caught.

She will come
in a radiance of new-made skin,
in a room of dying men
and dying flowers,
in the shadow of her large mother,
with her books propped up
& her ink-stained fingers,
lying back on pillows
white as blank pages,
laughing:
"I did it without
words!"

Elegy for Francis

Francis, the only pregnant white whale in captivity, died last night of internal poisoning in her tank at the New York Aquarium at Coney Island. . . .
   —*The New York Times*, May 26, 1974

Too big & too intelligent
to reproduce,
the ferns will outlast us,
not needing each other
with their dark spores,
& the cockroaches
with their millions of egg-cases,
& even the one-celled waltzers
dancing pseudopod to pseudopod,
but we are too big, too smart
to stick around.

Floating in Coney Island,
floating on her white belly—
while the fetus flips its flippers
in the womb
& she circles in the belly of the tank.

The last calf
beat her brains out
minutes after birth
& this one died unborn . . .

Fourteen months in the womb,
fourteen months to enter

the world of whaledom
through a tank in Coney Island.
Not worth it,
the calf decides,
& dies,
taking along its mother.

⚜

The whales are friendly, social animals
& produce big, brainy babies;
produce them one by one
in the deep arctic waters,
produce them painfully
through months of mating
& pregnancies that last
more than a year.

They croon to their unborn calves
in poetry—whale poetry
which only a few humans
have been privileged to hear.
Melville died for the privilege
& so will I
straining my ears
all the way to Coney Island.

⚜

Dear Francis, dead at ten
in your second pregnancy,
in the seventh year of captivity . . .
Was it weariness of the tank, the cage,
the zoo-prison of marriage?
Or was it loneliness—
the loneliness of pregnant whales?

Or was it nostalgia for the womb,
the arctic waste,
the belly of your own cold mother?

When a whale dies at sixteen hundred pounds
we must make big moans.
When a whale dies with an unborn baby
of one hundred and fifty pounds—
a small elegy is not enough;
we must weep loud enough
to be heard
all the way to Coney Island.

᪉

Why am I weeping
into *The New York Times*
for a big beluga whale
who could never have been
my sister?

Why am I weeping for a baby whale
who died happy
in the confines of the womb?

Because when the big-brained babies
die, we are all dying;
& the ferns live on
shivering
in the warm wind.

For Claudia, Against Narrowness

Narrowing life because of the fears,
narrowing it between the dust motes,
narrowing the pink baby
between the green-limbed monsters,
& the drooling idiots,
& the ghosts of Thalidomide infants,
narrowing hope,
always narrowing hope.

Mother sits on one shoulder hissing:
Life is dangerous.
Father sits on the other sighing:
Lucky you.
Grandmother, grandfather, big sister:
You'll die if you leave us,
you'll die if you ever leave us.

Sweetheart, baby sister,
you'll die anyway
& so will I.
Even if you walk the wide greensward,
even if you
& your beautiful big belly
embrace the world of men & trees,
even if you moan with pleasure,
& smoke the sweet grass
& feast on strawberries in bed,
you'll die anyway—
wide or narrow,
you're going to die.

As long as you're at it,
die wide.
Follow your belly to the green pasture.
Lie down in the sun's dapple.
Life is not as dangerous
as mother said.
It is more dangerous,
more wide.

For My Husband

You sleep in the darkness,
you with the back I love
& the gift of sleeping
through my noisy nights of poetry.

I have taken other men into my thoughts
since I met you.
I have loved parts of them.
But only you sleep on through the darkness
like a mountain where my house is planted,
like a rock on which my temple stands,
like a great dictionary holding every word—
even some
I have never spoken.

You breathe.
The pages of your dreams are riffled
by the winds of my writing.
The pillow creases your cheek
as I cover pages.

Element in which I swim
or fly,
silent muse, backbone, companion—
it is unfashionable
to confess to marriage—
yet I feel no bondage
in this air we share.

Cheever's People

These beautifully grown men. These hungerers.
Look at them looking!
They're overdrawn on all accounts but hope
& they've missed
(for the hundredth time) the express
to the city of dreams
& settled, sighing, for a desperate local;
so who's to blame them
if they swim through swimming pools of twelve-
year-old Scotch, or fall
in love with widows (other than their wives)
or suddenly can't ride
in elevators? In that suburb of elms
& crabgrass (to which
the angel banished them) nothing is more real
than last night's empties.

So, if they pack up, stuff their vitals
in a two-suiter,
& (with passports bluer than their eyes)
pose as barons
in Kitzbühel, or poets in Portofino,
something in us sails
off with them (dreaming of bacon-lettuce-
and-tomato sandwiches).
Oh, all the exiles of the twenties knew
that America
was discovered this way: desperate men,
wearing nostalgia
like a hangover, sailed out, sailed out

in search of passports,
eyes, an ancient kingdom, beyond the absurd
suburbs of the heart.

Dear Anne Sexton

On line at the supermarket
waiting for the tally,
the blue numerals
tattooed
on the white skins
of paper,
I read your open book
of folly
and take heart,
poet of my heart.

The poet as housewife!
Keeper of steak & liver,
keeper of keys, locks, razors,
keeper of blood & apples,
of breasts & angels,
Jesus & beautiful women,
keeper also of women
who are not beautiful--

you glide in from Cape Ann
on your winged broomstick—
the housewife's Pegasus.

You are sweeping the skies clear
of celestial rubbish.
You are placing a child there,
a heart here . . . .
You are singing for your supper.

Dearest wordmother & hunger-teacher,
full professor of courage,
dean of women
in my school of books,
thank you.

I have checked out
pounds of meat & cans of soup.
I walk home laden,
light with writing you.

Letter to Myselves

You can be hurt
because you want too much;
because in your face it says:
love me, nurture me;
because in your teeth it says:
sugar flows to us;
because in your tongue it says:
drive in the spike.

You can be hurt
because you care too much
because your ribs swing out like shutters
& your heart
glows like a night light.

You can be hurt
because you need too much
because your skin comes off in streamers
& your veins
twang like guitar strings.
You can be hurt that way.

You made your head
a wind tunnel for death.
You made your womb
the world's confessional.
You made your heart
a lump of burning clay.

You, me—
we can be hurt that way.

Dearest Man-in-the-Moon

Dearest man-in-the-moon,
ever since our lunch of cheese
& moonjuice
on the far side of the sun,
I have walked the craters of New York,
a trail of slime
ribboning between my legs,
a phosphorescent banner
which is tied to you,
a beam of moonlight
focused on your navel,
a silver chain
from which my body dangles,
& my whole torso chiming
like sleighbells in a Russian novel.

Dearest man-in-the-moon,
I used to fear moonlight
thinking her my mother.
I used to dread nights
when the moon was full.
I used to scream
"Pull down the shade!"
because the moonface leered at me,
because I felt her mocking,
because my fear lived in me
like rats in a wheel of cheese.

You have eaten out my fear.
You have licked

the creamy inside of my moon.
You have kissed
the final crescent of my heart
& made it full.

Dear Keats

FOR HOWARD MOSS

Already six years past your age!
The steps in Rome,
the house near Hampstead Heath,
& all your fears
that you might cease to be
before your pen had glean'd. . . .

My dear dead friend,
you were the first to teach me
how the dust could sing.
I followed in your footsteps
up the Heath.
I listened hard
for Lethe's nightingale.

& now at 31, I want to live.
Oblivion holds no adolescent charms.
& all the "souls of poets
dead & gone,"
& all the "Bards
of Passion & Mirth"
cannot make death—
its echo, its damp earth—
resemble birth.

*

You died in Rome—
in faltering sunlight—
Bernini's watery boat still sinking

in the fountain in the square below.
When Severn came to say
the roses bloomed,
you did not "glut thy sorrow,"
but you wept—
you wept for them
& for your posthumous life.

& yet we all lead posthumous lives somehow.
The broken lyre,
the broken lung,
the broken love.
Our names are writ in newsprint
if not water.

"Don't breathe on me—" you cried,
"it comes like ice."

❧

Last words.
(I can't imagine mine.
Perhaps some muttered dream,
some poem, some curse.)

Three months past 25,
you lived on milk.
They reeled you backward
in the womb of love.

❧

A tepid February Roman Spring.
Fruit trees in bloom;
& Hampstead still in snow

& Fanny Brawne receives a hopeful note
when you are two weeks dead.

A poet's life:
always awaiting mail.

❧

For God's sake
kick against the pricks!
There aren't very many roses.
Your life was like an hourglass
with no sand.
The words slid through
& rested under glass;
the flesh decayed
to moist Italian clay.

❧

At autopsy,
your lungs were wholly gone.
Was that from too much singing?
Too many rifts of ore?
You spent your life breath
breathing life in words.
But words return no breath
to those who write.

Letters, Life, & Literary Remains . . .

"I find that I cannot exist without poetry. . . ."

"O for a Life of Sensations rather than of Thoughts!"

"What the imagination seizes as Beauty must be truth. . . ."

"We hate poetry that has a palpable design upon us. . . ."

"Sancho will invent a Journey heavenwards as well as
     anybody. . . ."

"Poetry should be great and unobtrusive, a thing which
     enters into one's soul."

"Why should we kick against the Pricks when we can
     walk on Roses?"

"Axioms in philosophy are not axioms until they are
     proved upon our pulses. . . ."

"Until we are sick, we understand not. . . ."

"Sorrow is Wisdom. . . ."

"Wisdom is folly. . . ."

✤

Too wise
& yet not wise enough
at 25.
Sick, you understood
& understanding
were too weak to write.

Proved on the pulse: poetry.

If sorrow is wisdom
& wisdom folly

then too much sorrow
is folly.

I find that I cannot exist without sorrow
& I find that sorrow
cannot exist without poetry. . . .

What the imagination seizes as beauty
must be poetry. . . .

What the imagination seizes must be. . . .

❧

You claimed no lust for fame
& yet you burned.

"The faint conceptions I have of poems to come brings the
blood frequently into my forehead."

I burn like you
until it often seems
my blood will break
the boundaries of my brain
& issue forth in one tall fountain
from my skull.

❧

A spume of blood from the forehead: poetry.

A plume of blood from the heart: poetry.

Blood from the lungs: alizarin crimson words.

❧

"I will not spoil my love of gloom
by writing an Ode to Darkness. . . ."

The blood turns dark;
it stiffens on the sheet.
At night the childhood walls
are streaked with blood—
until the darkness seems awash with red
& children sleep behind two blood-branched lids.

❦

"My imagination is a monastery
& I am its monk. . . ."

At five & twenty,
very far from home,
death picked you up
& sorted to a pip.
& 15 decades later,
your words breathe:
syllables of blood.

A strange transfusion
for my feverish verse.

I suck your breath,
your rhythms & your blood,
& all my fiercest dreams are sighed away.

I send you love,
dear Keats,
I send you peace.

Since flesh can't stay
we keep the breath aloft.

Since flesh can't stay,
we pass the words along.

II / IN THE PENILE COLONY

*Literature cannot be the business
of a woman's life and it ought
not to be.*
　　　—ROBERT SOUTHEY
　　　　　TO CHARLOTTE BRONTË

*Women are at once the boldest and most
unmanageable revolutionaries.*
　　—EAMON DE VALERA

*It is written. A daughter is
a vain treasure to her father.
From anxiety about her he does
not sleep at night; during her
early years lest she be seduced,
in her adolescence lest she go
astray, in her marriageable
years lest she does not find
a husband, when she is married
lest she be childless, and when
she is old lest she practice
witchcraft.*
　　　—THE TALMUD

*But I was changing. Slowly, if you like,
but what matter? To change is the great
thing.*
　　—COLETTE

Becoming a Nun

FOR JENNIFER JOSEPHY

On cold days
it is easy to be reasonable,
to button the mouth against kisses,
dust the breasts
with talcum powder
& forget
the red pulp meat
of the heart.

On those days
it beats
like a digital clock—
not a beat at all
but a steady whirring
chilly as green neon,
luminous as numerals in the dark,
cool as electricity.

& I think:
I can live without it all—
love with its blood pump,
sex with its messy hungers,
men with their peacock strutting,
their silly sexual baggage,
their wet tongues in my ear
& their words like little sugar suckers
with sour centers.

On such days
I am zipped in my body suit,

I am wearing seven league red suede boots,
I am marching over the cobblestones
as if they were the heads of men,

& I am happy
as a seven-year-old virgin
holding Daddy's hand.

Don't touch.
Don't try to tempt me with your ripe persimmons.
Don't threaten me with your volcano.
The sky is clearer when I'm not in heat,
& the poems
are colder.

Empty

. . . who shall measure the heat and violence of the poet's heart when caught and tangled in a woman's body?
—VIRGINIA WOOLF

Every month,
the reminder of emptiness
so that you are tuned
to your bodyharp,
strung out on the harpsichord
of all your nerves
& hammered bloody blue
as the crushed fingers
of the woman pianist
beaten by her jealous lover.

Who was she?
Someone I invented
for this poem,
someone I imagined . . .

Never mind,
she is me, you—

tied to that bodybeat,
fainting on that rack of blood,
moving to that metronome—
empty, empty, empty.

No use.
The blood is thicker

than the roots of trees,
more persistent than my poetry,
more baroque than her bruised music.
It gilds the sky above the Virgin's head.
It turns the lilies white.

Try to run:
the blood still follows you.
Swear off children,
seek a quiet room
to practice your preludes & fugues.
Under the piano,
the blood accumulates;
eventually it floats you both away.

Give in.
Babies cry & music is your life.
Darling, you were born to bleed
or rock.
& the heart breaks
either way.

Egyptology

I am the Sphinx.
I am the woman buried in sand
up to her chin.
I am waiting for an archaeologist
to unearth me,
to dig out my neck & my nipples,
bare my claws
& solve my riddle.

No one has solved my riddle
since Oedipus.

&

I face the pyramids which rise
like angular breasts
from the dry body of Egypt.
My fertile river is flowing down below—
a lovely lower kingdom.
Every woman should have a delta
with such rich silt—
brown as the buttocks
of Nubian queens.

&

O friend, why have you come to Egypt?
Aton & Yahweh
are still feuding.
Moses is leading his people
& speaking of guilt.

The voice out of the volcano
will not be still.

&

A religion of death,
a woman buried alive.
For thousands of years
the sand drifted over my head.
My sex was a desert,
my hair more porous than pumice,
& nobody sucked my lips
to make me tell.

&

The pyramid breasts, though huge,
will never sag.
In the center of each one,
a king lies buried.
In the center of each one,
a darkened chamber . . .
a tunnel,
dead men's bones,
malignant gold.

Wrinkles

FOR NAOMI LAZARD

> *Sometimes I can't wait until I look*
> *like Nadezhda Mandelstam.*
> —NAOMI LAZARD

My friends are tired.
The ones who are married are tired
of being married.
The ones who are single are tired
of being single.

They look at their wrinkles.
The ones who are single attribute their wrinkles
to being single.
The ones who are married attribute their wrinkles
to being married.

They have very few wrinkles.
Even taken together,
they have very few wrinkles.
But I cannot persuade them
to look at their wrinkles
collectively.
& I cannot persuade them that being married
or being single
has nothing to do with wrinkles.

Each one sees a deep & bitter groove,
a San Andreas fault across her forehead.
"It is only a matter of time

before the earthquake."
They trade the names of plastic surgeons
like recipes.

My friends are tired.
The ones who have children are tired
of having children.
The ones who are childless are tired
of being childless.

They love their wrinkles.
If only their wrinkles were deeper
they could hide.

Sometimes I think
(but do not dare to tell them)
that when the face is left alone to dig its grave,
the soul is grateful
& rolls in.

Self-Portrait

She was not a slender woman,
but her skin was milk
mixed in with strawberry jam
& between her legs the word *purple* was born
& her hair was the color of wheat & yellow butter.

Her eyes were dark as the North Atlantic sea.

She learned the untranslatable words of dawn.
She studied her own fear & wrote its verses.
She used the hole in her heart to play wind-music.
She built her book-houses over her empty cellar.

She nursed on the muse at first,
then became her own mother.

Statue

Cement up to the neck
& my head packed
with unsaid words.
A gullet full of pebbles,
a mouth
of cast concrete—
I am stuck
in a lovelessness so thick,
it seems my natural element.
My mouth closes
on stones.

Hand frozen to my chin,
my back a question mark,
my heart soldered
to its arteries,
my feet planted
in grass that cannot grow,
The Thinker ponders
ten more years of this:
a woman
living the life
of a statue.

Break free!
Melt the metal
in love's cauldron,
open doors, eyes, heart,
those frozen ventricles,
those stuck tongues,
those stuttering dependencies.

When the statue walks,
will the world dissolve?
When she shakes her shoulders,
will the sky shrug
& skitter off in space?

Or will the clouds cluster
to cover her,
& the blue wind gather
at her shoulders
& the men streak by
like jet trails in the air,
utterly ephemeral?

Parable of the Four-Poster

Because she wants to touch him,
she moves away.
Because she wants to talk to him,
she keeps silent.
Because she wants to kiss him,
she turns away
& kisses a man she does not want to kiss.

He watches
thinking she does not want him.
He listens
hearing her silence.
He turns away
thinking her distant
& kisses a girl he does not want to kiss.

They marry each other—
a four-way mistake.
He goes to bed with his wife
thinking of her.
She goes to bed with her husband
thinking of him.
—& all this in a real old-fashioned four-poster bed.

Do they live unhappily ever after?
Of course.
Do they undo their mistakes ever?
Never.
Who is the victim here?
Love is the victim.
Who is the villain?
Love that never dies.

Mute Marriages

Mute marriages:
the ten-ton block of ice
obstructing the throat, the heart,
the red filter of the liver,
the clogged life.

It is a glacier
in which frozen children swim
ground round with boulders,
pebbles, bits of stone
from other ice ages.

Here a lapis glitters,
here a shard of bottle glass—
valuables & junk:
the history of a house
told in its garbage cans,
the history of a life
in its nightmares.

Speak the dream.
Follow the red thread
of the images.
Defrost the glacier
with the live heat
of your breath,
propelled by the heart's
explosion.

Playing with the Boys

All the boring tedious young men
with dead eyes & dirty hair . . .
all the mad young men who hate their mothers,
all the squalling baby boys . . .

have grown up
& now write book reviews
or novels about the life
of the knife-fighter,
or movies in which grown men
torture each other—

all the squalling boring baby boys!

I am not part of their game.
I have no penis.
I have a pen, two eyes
& I bleed monthly.

When the moon shines on the sea
I see the babies
riding on moonwaves
asking to be born.

Does everything else in nature hate
its mother?
Does the chick fling
bits of eggshell at the hen?
Does the pear spit
its seeds against the pear tree?

Who *made* all these squalling baby boys?

I am a reasonable, hardworking woman.
I sit at my desk & write
from eight to three.
When I emerge I do not ask your blessing.
What have I done but bleed
to get your curse?

Sexual Soup

A man so sick that the sexual soup
cannot save him—

the chicken soup of sex
which cures everything:
tossed mane of noodles,
bits of pale white meat.
the globules of yellow fat
like love . . .

But he is a man so sick
no soup can save him.

His throat has healed into a scar.
Rage fills his guts.
He wants to diet on dust.

I offered to feed him
(spoon by spoon)
myself.

I offered my belly as a bowl.
I offered my hands as spoons,
my knees as tongs,
my breasts as the chafing dish
to keep us warm.

I offered my navel
as a brandy snifter.

"My tongue is gone," he said,
"I have no teeth.
My mouth is with my mother in the grave.
I've offered up my hunger to the air,
my nostrils to the wind,
my sex to death,
my eyes to nothingness & dust."

"What do you lust for then?"
I asked.

"I lust for nothing."

Colder

He was six feet four, and forty-six,
and even colder than he thought he
was.

     —JAMES THURBER,
       The Thirteen Clocks

Not that I cared about the other women.
Those perfumed breasts with hearts
of pure rock salt.
Lot's wives—
all of them.

I didn't care
if they fondled him at parties,
eased him in at home
between a husband & a child,
sucked him dry
with vacuum cleaner kisses.

It was the coldness that I minded,
though he'd warned me.
"I'm cold," he said—
(as if that helped any).
But he was colder
than he thought he was.

Cold sex.
A woman has to die
& be exhumed
four times a week
to know the meaning of it.

His hips are razors,
his pelvic bones are knives,
even his elbows could cut butter.

Cold flows from his mouth
like a cloud of carbon dioxide.
His penis is pure dry ice
which turns to smoke.
His face hangs over my face—
an ice carving.

One of these days
he'll shatter
or
he'll melt.

The End

The congealed snow
of an old love affair.

A fistful of water—
& my hand closed
to contain you.

Still,
you leak through.

Where have you gone to?
What spring has thawed
the ice around my heart?

Old refrigerator
with your door pried off,
you bake in the sun.

I open my hand
& my palm gleams pink
as a peppermint lozenge.

There are dry old riverbeds,
a lifeline
deep as sleep.

There are beads of sweat—
all mine.

There is no more trace
of you.

Sylvia Plath Is Alive in Argentina

Not dead.
Oh sisters, Alvarez lied,
& Hughes lied,
& even Harper & Row
(I am sorry to say)
lied.

She did not die.
They buried a waxworks doll.
Sylvia Plath is alive in Argentina!

& she sits playing chess
with Diane Arbus
& exchanging sleeping pills
with Norma Jean
& giggling in the dark
with Zelda Sayre.

A regular girls' dormitory
down there
in Argentina.
The crazy ladies
having the last laugh—

while their martyr stock
goes up like Fairchild Camera
& their sisters moan & sigh:
Men did them in.

"Don't cry.
Don't mourn for us at all,
dear sisters.

We're happiest down here
in Argentina.
We're happier down here
than up in hell.

The divine Marquis makes love
with so much sweetness,
& Hitler is the daddy we never had.
We live quite peacefully among the exiled tyrants.
What makes you say that men must *all* be bad?"

Chastity

FOR KRISTIN BOOTH GLEN

The sperm-smell of the mango
reminds me of how long it's been
since a man opened me up
& sucked my juice,
the sum of my parts
made hole.

*

I belong to a curious cult
of singing nuns.
We all have padlocked thighs
& knotted knees.
We work the beehive for ink
instead of honey.
& we hum like lovers coming
as we work.

*

Chastity!
Only the rankest sensualist
gives up sex.
The others never have to.
Men open me up too wide,
too desolate.
I've sworn off desolation.

*

The mango is a messy fruit to eat.
It covers the front of your dress

with yellow juice.
& strings of mango
hang between your teeth.
& all you're left with
is
a slimy pit.

Distrusting advice—
there is no one she wants to be
but herself—
although sometimes
she wishes
herself dead.

Who can tell her how to live?
Ms. Lonelyhearts—
with her heap of red letters?
Doctor X—
with his couch shaped
like a coffin?
Mr. Sex—
gimlet-eyed
cock-of-the-walk,
with his cakewalks & tangos,
his mangoes & bitter persimmons,
his helium balloons
bursting on branches
& his condoms
that glow in the dark?

No.
She turns her back.
Mistakes: she will make them
herself.
Love: she will choose,
like the rest of us,

badly.
Death: it will come
when it will come.

& Life: not reasoned or easy
but at least
her own.

The Woman of It

Your slit so like mine:
the woman of it,
the warm womanwide of thigh,
& the comfort of it—
knowing your nipples like mine,
& the likeness of it,
watching the mirror make love,
& the lovematch:
the mirror of you
in me.

I have creamed my hands
in the cave;
I have known my mother.
Years to get past
the barrier reefs of words.
We were natural together
as two little girls in the bath.
We hoped to be women someday,
we hoped to grow up.

Menstruation in May

Deaths & betrayals,
a friend having her breasts cut off,
a friend having his heart re-wired,
a husband lying,
a lover never writing,
& all this in the middle of May.

I walk out into the green wind of Spring.
The air whistles at my calves
like silk stockings—
my grandmother's silk stockings
kept in a drawer—
& whispering songs of the twenties.

My breasts ache,
my heart skips over cracks,
my womb pulls earthward
with its heavy blood.
I seem to be attached to those I love
by chains of flesh.
Perhaps the mind lacks empathy enough;
the body has to bleed as well.

⚜

I can't imagine them cutting you apart—
I with my endless dreams of torture,
who lay awake nights with my eyelids screaming
all childhood long.

I never saw your breasts
yet can't imagine you without them.

All week I have been fondling my nipples,
half in terror, half in pleasure.
Stay, flesh, stay.
If it is all we have,
especially,
stay.

*

Is there a poetry of blood
where lines are arms lopped off
& stanzas are whole bodies opened wide?
Is there an art which pains us
just like life?

I squeeze my breast
for the invisible ink of milk.
I bear down hard—
no baby's head appears.

The poems keep flowing monthly
like my blood.

The word is flesh, I say,
still unconvinced.

The flesh is flesh.
The word is on its own.

Fugue for Three Hands & Ornate Bedstead

FOR JILL ROBINSON

> *The only way for a relationship to survive,*
> *I think, is to have no sex at all. After*
> *all, you marry for friendship, for compan-*
> *ionship—and passion after a while . . .*
> *pfffft. I mean, does it excite you when*
> *your left hand touches your right?*
> —DIANE VON UND ZU FÜRSTENBERG,
> *New York* Magazine, February 5, 1973

Pfffft.
My left hand is touching my right
after seven years
of marriage.

Donne's lovers' hands
cemented by their sweat
the stars of star-crossed lovers
whose life-lines
cross each other out—
could not be more electric
than these hands
making love from left to right

I hate to come right out & say this
& seem dull,
but I get excited
when my left hand strokes my right.

The right hand holds the pen
& feels the cramp,

while the cool & lucid
sinister left hand
makes love with silent finger-pads & palm
& helps the other write.

What friendship
after years of breaking bread!
These hands have gone to table
& to bed
for seven years
& they are still not severed.

They sweat, they freeze, they chap,
they crack their knuckles.
They tie each other's ties.
& buckle buckles.
& yet these hands are friends
when all is done
& when it comes to passion
they aren't numb.

Occasionally, it's true,
one needs a friend—
a hairy, unfamiliar
helping hand.

If two is company
can three be ecstasy?

But what is the sound
of three hands clapping?

Birth & Other Endings

1

The madonna's face
at the annunciation:
slightly appalled,
reluctant, sad, resigned.

That life should come through us
is not always pleasing:
we are not whole enough
to risk that split.

Like Polish dolls
that open into others,
we cannot comprehend
the self as toy.

2

Yet she consulted her body:
it was time.

3 (CHANT FOR AN AMBIVALENT LADY AT IMPLANTATION)

Lovebud,
pinkworm,
pinking shears
for my crooked life,
fleshknot,
loveknot,
small smiler,
hookworm.

4

What dies twice
inside you:

      the cells
      & then the sons of cells . . .

sperm of moonlight,
tendrils of moonmelon . . .

      all his hands on your body
      cascading,
      all his hands of water
      making water music
      on your marble breasts

      cannot erase
      that twice-dying death,
      that lonely wholeness
      of the cell
      that cannot divide.

5 (THE EYE OF TIME, AFTER PAUL CELAN)

The eye of time
is not cross-eyed,
but a great weeping cunt
out of which corpses come,
wept for before conception.

The weeping eye of time
is orgasm & mourning
both at once.

It holds a constant wake—
& never sleeps.

Oh great female eye
from which men proceed
like visions
yet imagine themselves real—
will you never blink?

Will you never lose
an eyelash to the sun?

Will you never
send your tears to reach the moon,
& fill the dead sea
of fertility?

6 (PREGNANT ON THE NUDE BEACH)

Friends falling off the edges of the earth—
as if the world had suddenly gone flat,
& just by walking carelessly
they'd slipped,
naked
in the North Atlantic sea.

Conspirators against the sea,
cocky in our deathward nakedness,
denying twilight & denying dark,
denying flatness.

7 (INSIDE THE CAVE)

The cave opens
to call me in.

I am the woman
who has sown the whirlwind,
& the voice I hear
is my own child-voice
screaming of milk
in the dark.

It is so dark dark dark.
The darkness moves along my spine
like lightning.
The thousand eggs I have betrayed,
the twenty children
that I might have had
in twenty years of blood
all call to me at once. . . .

Their mouths are clots of blood.
Their skins are crimson
as a sadist's dream.
Their voices are as angry
& as red
as a first day's flow.

Everything I see is red!
I dream watermelon dreams
of houses
with translucent ruby walls.
Every night I curl up
in sleep's womb
& hope the darkness seeds.

Come in a shower of golden rain!
Come in a cloud of snow or milk—
a milky mouthful

white as a page of poems,
but without the words.

Penis Envy

I envy men who can yearn
with infinite emptiness
toward the body of a woman,

hoping that the yearning
will make a child,
that the emptiness itself
will fertilize the darkness.

Women have no illusions about this,
being at once
houses, tunnels,
cups & cupbearers,
knowing emptiness as a temporary state
between two fullnesses,
& seeing no romance in it.

If I were a man
doomed to that infinite emptiness,
& having no choice in the matter,
I would, like the rest, no doubt,
find a woman
& christen her moonbelly,
madonna, gold-haired goddess
& make her the tent of my longing,
the silk parachute of my lust,
the blue-eyed icon of my sacred sexual itch,
the mother of my hunger.

But since I am a woman,
I must not only inspire the poem

but also type it,
not only conceive the child
but also bear it,
not only bear the child
but also bathe it,
not only bathe the child
but also feed it,
not only feed the child
but also carry it
everywhere, everywhere . . .

while men write poems
on the mysteries of motherhood.

I envy men who can yearn
with infinite emptiness.

Cold Comfort to a Man with a Growing Daughter

FOR JOHN UPDIKE

Rueful
(& a trifle
lewd),
the youngish old
man
falls
in love
with ladies
of his own
creation:
characters
in books he writes
&
(even)
daughters.

As if
the leaping act
of love,
the spill of sperm
across that tiny
sky
(within the vaulting
universe
of womb)
were like
the nimble fingers
on the keys
spattering specks of black

on milky
bond.

Oh oldish
youngish saddish
father,
lugubrious
(yet funny) author,
man of many
sweet imaginary
daughters—
do not curse
the man
who fucks
your daughter.
You stole another
old man's laughter,
too.
& besides,
she is probably
only thinking of
you.

In the Penile Colony

FOR BOB PHILLIPS

Wearing my familiar worry wrapped
around me like a fur coat,
I walk out into the transatlantic air,
endangered species,
womankind in a world
of shivering men.

Kindness, worry, anxiousness-to-please
have been my nursemaids;
fear has suckled me
since I first learned to breathe.

But now the streets are strewn with beggarmen
who kneel
clutching tin cups & pencils,
strutting on their stumps
where legs once grew.

This is a curious world
changing so fast
that we are all babies
born in taxicabs.

That first great gust of air
which fills our lungs
turns blood from iron red
to inky black—
& never back.

A street of stumps?
A forest thick with cocks?
"Alice lost in the penile colony"—
you said.
But the forest is dying
(Uncle Vanya knew)
& see how those trees
bend & whimper
under their own dry rot.

Dying,
they want to kill us.
("Don't take it personally,"
the murderer said.)

We women will have to shed
our wraps of fear.
Kindness, worry, anxiousness-to-please
are luxuries our kind can no more wear
than fur coats.

In a rotting forest,
we are lumberjacks
raising our double axes. . . .

III / HUNGERING

> "*I want to be first!*
> *I want to be liked!*"
> *(You can't get one and keep*
> *the other.)*
> —ENID BAGNOLD

I've had better times of course—the
halcyon days, rings, ringlets, ashes
of roses, shit, chantilly, high teas,
drop scones, serge suits, binding
attachments, all that.
> —EDNA O'BRIEN

I want a classic purity, where
dung is dung and angels are
angels.
> —HENRY MILLER

Tapestry, with Unicorn

What we were searching for
did not, of course, exist—
that tapestried morning,
under those woven clouds
where impossible birds
sang quite incredibly
of unattainable things.

A moth among the dandelions
warbled like the nightingale of Keats,
& trochees sang among the iambs,
while you in your curled collar & brocaded vest,
were beaming down the sun-strewn silken grass
where I lay in a frenzy of ruffles,
ear pressed to the earth
so I might hear—
the echoing hoofbeats of the unicorn.

He came in a blaze
of embroidered glory, with agate eyes
and his infamous ivory horn
blaring baroque concerti—
& thinking to have captured him for good,
we toasted in white wine and wafers,
and took, before witnesses,
impossible vows.

The rest you know:
how in the toadstool damp of evening
where lovers toss and cough,
speaking to each other

in the thick syllables of sleep,
through the long winter's night of marriage,
the unicorn slips away,
& love, like an insomniac's nightmare,
becomes only
the lesser of two evils.

Sometimes he comes again,
thrashing through the tapestried dark,
uprooting limbs & sheets
& finespun wisps of hair.
But the quest having been forgotten,
we do not know him,
or else we call him
by a different name.

The Poet Writes in I

The poet writes in *I*
because she knows
no other language.

We is a continent,
& a poet must be
an island.

She is an inlet.
He is a peninsula.
They is the great engulfing sea.

The poet writes in *I*
as the clock
strikes on metal,

as the bee wing
flies on honey,
as trees are rooted
in the sky.

I is the language
of the poet's inner chantings:
a geography of sadness,

a metronome of pain,
a map of elevations
in the jungled heart.

You Whom I Hoped to Reach by Writing

You whom I hoped to reach by writing,
you beyond the multicolored tangle
of telephone wires,
you with your white paper soul
trampled in transit,
you with kaleidoscope stamps
& black cancellations,
you who put your finger on my heart as I slept,
you whom I jostle in elevators,
you whom I stare at in subways,
you shopping for love in department stores . . .

I write to you
& someone else answers:
the man who hates his wife
& wants to meet me,
the girl who mistakes me for mother. . . .
My strange vocation
is to be paid for my nightmares.

I write to you, my love,
& someone else
always answers.

She Leaps

She leaps into the alien heart
of the passerby, the drunk,
the girl who spouts Freudian talk
over Szechuan food.

She is part herself,
part everyone.
"Thank you for writing the story of my life,"
her mash notes read.
& "Can you tell me how to leave my husband?"
& "Can you tell me how to find a husband?"
& "Can you tell me how to write,
or how to feel,
or how to save my life?"

She knows nothing
but how to leap.
She has no answers for herself
or anyone.

One foot after another,
she flies through the air. . . .

She leaps over cracks
& breaks
her father's back.

In Praise of Clothes

If it is only for the taking off—
    the velvet cloak,
    the ostrich feather boa,
    the dress which slithers to the floor
    with the sound of strange men sighing
    on imagined street corners . . .

If it is only for the taking off—
    the red lace bra
    (with rosewindows of breasts),
    the red lace pants
    (with dark suggestion
    of Venus' first name),
    the black net stockings
    cobwebby as fate,
    the black net stockings
    crisscrossed like our lives,
    the silver sandals
    glimmering as rain—

clothes are necessary.

Oh bulky barrier between soul & soul,
soul & self—
how it comforts us
to take you down!
How it heartens us to strip you off!

    & this is no matter of fashion.

Spring × 2

Pink-green spring,
I have put my tongue
between your baby lips,
put my ear against your pale green chest,
& felt the small persistent pulse
surge in your heart of lettuce-green,
beat in your weed-slim wrist,
stare out of your apple-yellow eyes
until the world was gold.

Spring,
there is a silver triangle
inside your heart,
the smell of earth inside your head,
& all this sudden tenderness of mine
for blades of grass.

What do these blades cut?
My words?

Spring,
you are a pinking shears: you cut
fresh edges on the world.

II

Spring being pink & green
& my body being strung tight
with wanting you
& the sheets of my bed being pink & green

I lay down with you in imagination
& ran away from you
in life.

The whole park was pink & green
& we rode in a yellow taxi drenched
with rain
& my glasses were fogged with spring rain
& wanting you
till I ran away.

Missionary love
comes to savage me
in jungle spring!

Bringing Christian charity
(with a Jewish accent)
bringing deciduous erections
& water everywhere
(because I am afraid of fire).

Chief curator in my sad museum,
ethnologist, explorer—
pole up my amazon river.
Civilize me—
if you can.

In the Middle

Because my grandfather
pulled love out of his gut
like taffy,
mixed it with bile
& covered canvases with it,
I write to you now:
a woman in the middle of her life,
with one foot in the past
& one foot in the future
& a husband I dug for
all the way to China.

I write to you
out of a roiling gut,
chronic insomnia
& bad dreams.
Once, I *prayed* to be a poet—
before I knew the price.

Fear is the main means of transportation.
Fear propels the pen across the page.
Fear pulls me out of bed at night to write.
Fear drags me screaming "No!"
into your arms.

I catch love like a disease:
it hits me broadside in the gut—a soccer ball.
The first sure sign of love
is diarrhea.

& you, my friend,
an unpeeled Mexican fruit.

Or else a hookworm
hooking in my heart,
a fungus living in the Eden of my skin,
a boil on the bone of my forehead
thinking of you,
a stubborn, unscratchable itch
inside my cunt.

Oh that unscratchability lament!
Oh those bothersome, boring hookworm blues!
Oh that itch, that howling bitch in heat!
Oh that bookworm's wail: *I want to live!*

The worm has turned,
the fat is in the fire.
Your cat is into my bag,
my heart's for hire.

I suppose I'll have to love you
at this rate.
In the middle of my life:
too soon, too late.

Sunjuice

What happens when the juice of the sun
drenches you
with its lemony tang, its tart sweetness
& your whole body stings with singing
so that your toes sing to your mouth
& your navel whistles to your breasts
& your breasts wave to everyone
as you walk down the summer street?

What will you do
when nothing will do
but to throw your arms around trees
& men
& to greet every woman as sister
& to run naked in the spray of the fire hydrants
with children of assorted colors?

Will you cover your drenched skin
with woolen clothes?
Will you wear a diaper of herringbone tweed?
Will you piece together a shroud of figleaves
& lecture at the University
on the Lives of the Major Poets,
the History of Despair in Art?

Insomnia & Poetry

Sweet muse
with bitter milk,
I have lain
between your breasts,
put my ear
to your sea-shell-whispering navel,
& strained the salty marshes
of your sex
between my milk teeth.
Then I've slept at last,
my teeming head
against your rocking thigh.

Gentle angry mother
poetry,
where could I turn
from the terror of the night
but to your sweet maddening
ambivalence?
Where could I rest
but in your hurricane?
Who would always take me home
but you,
sweeping off the sooty stoop
of your wind-filled shack
on the edge
of the volcano?

Catching Up

We sit on a rock
to allow our souls
to catch up with us.

We have been traveling
a long time.

Behind us are forests of books
with pages green as leaves.
A blood sun stares
over the horizon.

Our souls are slow.
They walk miles behind
our long shadows.

They do not dance.
They need all their strength
merely to follow us.

Sometimes we run too fast
or trip climbing
the rotten rungs
in fame's ladder.

Our souls know
it leads nowhere.

They are not afraid
of losing us.

The Stone People

The people who do not quite care
about living,
who go on dragging their bodies around
out of habit,
who fill their mouths
without hunger,
who walk without any real destination,
who make love without love
& hate without rancor—
because, after all, they are only alive
by chance,
because, after all, they never asked
to be born,
because, after all, they do not follow
their stars.

They are the stone people.
Their skin is the color of shadows.
They stand as amazed as statues in a sculptor's
        courtyard.
They do not want your love.
It cannot save them.

Sometimes on planes which are crashing
they are the ones
who sing thinly as the engines flame.
You find their corpses smiling after car wrecks.
You find their frozen smiles beneath the snow.

Now I am opening my hand
to the air & water.

Now I am losing even the memory of pain.
Now my hand forgets
how to make a fist.
Now I am easy,
death is in my palm.

Unblocked

I had not written a poem in months,
my mouth was dry,
full of old newspaper clippings
& book reviews
& articles on the Sum Total
of Art.

Dead,
unable to write,
I had become my critics.
My passion was punished
with staleness,
my lust had turned
to printer's ink
on dust.

Then you appeared,
seized me quite suddenly
one night in the midst of a lecture,
bound my hands with rubber bands,
paper-clipped my nipples,
wrote your terrible lust on my belly,
your tenderness on my cheeks.

I felt that fatal spasm of love
& lost my dinner.
I felt that hunger for you
& I had diarrhea.

Oh, I know my cynical readers,
my cynical selves . . .

but the Muse winged over the toilet
& smelled the shit.
& the Muse flew up my ass
that fateful night
& now I am sick again
& now can write.

The Hole

She is frightened when the book is done.
The novel whose scrawled yellow pages
have filled her heart for seven years
is snatched away.
& the hole in her heart echoes
like a garbage can
thrown against a courtyard
in New York.

She writes to fill that hole
whose quicksand edges
eat her heart out from the muddy center,
& when they take away her pages,
her stuffing, her asbestos insulation,
she rattles
like a palsied hand
sticking out a silver spoon
for sugar.

The book-in-progress
was the mattress of a bed
where her past made love
to her future,
where her mother hugged her father,
where all the apparitions of the dead
slept like babies
after nighttime bottles.

She has no choice—she will begin again.
Her loneliness: the motor of her pen.

Tachycardia

In the chest is a caged bat
who seeks escape
through the mouth.

He flaps his wings
& the molars shiver.

He flaps his wings
& the thyroid bulges
like a snake
that has swallowed
a mouse.

He flaps his wings
uttering shrill cries
heard only by the ears
of the teeth.

He wants to soar
into the great world.
He is blind
as a bat.

You must convince him
that the chest
is a cradle
& a room
with a view.

Past the tonsils
lies terror.

Past the teeth
lies death.
Past the lips
lie lies,

lies, lies.

The Insomniac Talks to God

Staring eye insomnia
in the middle of the night,
the eye open
in the heart,

the chest's retina
flooded

& light wounding
the milkless nipples.

Sleep recedes
like a missed train.

Life, which is anyway
a long night without blinking,
a night which an eyelid
can obliterate,
shrinks to a point of light
on an open eyeball.

Terror writes poetry,
hope, prose.

I rise in the night
led by the single staring eye
which peers from my chest,
& begin to write.

Dear God:
I have found what I wanted

& find
I was wrong to want it.

The odd species I belong to
fears death
& in its fear
brings death everywhere.

Let me not be like them.

Let me not be.

Let be.

Eating Death, For Anne Sexton

My dearest Anne,
I am living by a lake
with a young man
I met one week after you died.

His beard is red,
his eyes flicker like cat's eyes,
& the amazing plum of his tongue
sweetens my brain.
He is like nobody
since I love him.
His cock sinks deep
in my heart.

❧

I have owed you a letter
for months.

❧

I wanted to chide
the manner of your death
the way I might have once
revised your poem.
You are like nobody
since I love you,
& you are gone.

❧

Can you believe
your death gave birth to me?
Live or die,

you said insistently.
You chose the second
& the first chose me.
I mourned you
& I found him
in one week.

*

Is love the sugar-coated poison
that gets us in the end?
We spoke of men
as often as of poems.
We tried to legislate away
the need for love—
that backseat fuck
& death caressing you.

*

Why did you do it
in your mother's coat?
(I know
but also know
I have to ask.)
Our mothers get us hooked,
then leave us cold,
all full-grown orphans
hungering after love.

*

You loved a man who spoke
"like greeting cards."
"He fucks me well
but I can't talk to him."

We shared that awful need
to talk in bed.
Love wasn't love
if we could only speak
in tongues.

❧

& the intensity of unlove
increased
until the motor, the running motor
could no longer power
the driver,
& you, with miles to go,
would rather sleep.

❧

Between the pills, the suicide pills
& our giggly vodkas in the Algonquin . . .
Between your round granny glasses
& your eyes blue as glaciers . . .
Between your stark mother-hunger
& your mother courage,
you knew there was only one poem
we all were writing.

❧

No competition.
"The poem belongs to everyone
& God."
I jumped out of your
suicide car
& into his arms.

Your death was mine.
I ate it
& returned.

❦

Now I sit by a lake
writing to you.
I love a man
who makes my fingers ache.
I type to you
off somewhere in the clouds.
I tap the table
like a spiritualist.

❦

Sex is a part of death;
that much I know.
Your voice was earth,
your eyes were glacier-blue.
Your slender torso
& long-stemmed American legs
drape across
this huge blue western sky.

❦

I want to tell you "Wait,
don't do it yet."
Love is the poison, Anne,
but love eats death.

ABOUT THE AUTHOR

ERICA JONG is the author of two previous books of poetry, *Fruits & Vegetables* (1971) and *Half-Lives* (1973), as well as *Fear of Flying*, published in 1973. She is currently at work on a new novel, *How to Save Your Own Life*, and a new collection of poems.